One Long Poem

Other books by William Harmon

Treasury Holiday (Poetry)
Legion: Civic Choruses (Poetry)
The Intussusception of Miss Mary America (Poetry)
Time in Ezra Pound's Work
The Oxford Book of American Light Verse

One Long Poem

WILLIAM HARMON

LOUISIANA STATE UNIVERSITY PRESS

BATON ROUGE AND LONDON

1982

Some of these pieces in more or less their present form have been in the *Agni Review*, the *Carolina Quarterly*, the *Cincinnati Poetry Review*, *Occum Ridge Review*, *Pebble*, *Shankpainter*, and the *Southern Poetry Review*. To their editors I want to record here my gratitude for accepting the things in the first place and for granting permission to reprint.

Other debts of gratitude are suggested by dedications or internal references: my mother, Virginia; my daughter Sally and son Will; friends Max Steele, James Seay, Kathleen Norris, and Norman Maclean. Still others, not mentioned out loud but nevertheless present as friends of the work, are Carolyn Kizer, George Starbuck, Robert Kirkpatrick, A. R. Ammons, Sam Carmack, Louis Simpson, and Albert Goldbarth.

Publication of this book has been supported by
a grant from the National Endowment for the Arts
in Washington, D.C., a federal agency.

DESIGNER: Albert Crochet
TYPEFACE: Linotron Electra
TYPESETTER: G & S Typesetters, Inc.
PRINTER: Thomson-Shore, Inc.
BINDER: John H. Dekker & Sons, Inc.

LIBRARY OF CONGRESS CATALOGING IN PUBLICATION DATA

Harmon, William, 1938–
    One long poem.

    I. Title.
PS3558.A624606   1982   811'.54   82-7213
ISBN 0-8071-1026-4   AACR2
ISBN 0-8071-1027-2 (pbk.)

Contents

Contents

One Long Poem

A Dawn Horse

Again the time and blood consuming sun crosses its corner
With a web of new born light
And there the last stars literally starve.

Grey among a hundred or so other greys
The dawn horse stirs,

Wakes to the waking manifold of new circumstance
And—totally inhuman and remote
Among deep empty drums of sound unreeling hungrily
As though long drowned or long ago
Among unsteady equinoctial darknesses—
Stands.

On the welcoming west slope of the world's first mountain
Half dark in the tilted dominion of imperial light and common grasses
He is standing up
As dew will stand on the difficult pitched deck of grass
In the looking light,

An ordinary model of simplicity,
Spotted
(As when water spots a smooth leaf
With many magnifying lenses
That evaporate in place
Or else slip·in the inflammatory turn and sloping),
Cold,
Solid enough for anybody.

Not one that waits at a fence for forked hay
Or feedbag of fodder hung on a headstall in a stable,
It is only he,
The ghostly dawn horse,

Not maiden white but stone colored,
Not a martingale gnawing nightmare
Or rainbow shouldered unicorn at allegorical attention
Or one of those things with wings

But a shaking shadow
Like the remote beating of the timed beast heart
Begotten and blessed by something blooded and blood loving;

Lowering his head for a moment
He starts to step.

The Dragon-Fire-Priest

Straight (dear mother)
The chain of jewels reaches from the sun
To the celebrant's heart
And when at midnight lamentation or noon thanksgiving
He opens his mouth to sing
The many-colored light there born becomes our holy litany
And the Dragonwords so become our holy harmony
That the perfect spun chain of jewels, returning,
Reaches from here as far again as the orbit of the woven sun himself,
To, fro,
And the execution of that pattern (dear
Mother) establishes the figure of the dance.

The nuns dance, the mothers dance, and the old men
Dance in the darkling light falling
Between the wine and the moon;
The belles dance between the old men and the moon
Until the moon, dead overhead at midnight himself, changes the dance,
The dance changes, the wives and husbands change in changed time.

The priest is a king, his song the key,
An ancient secret that accompanied the ancestors
When they traveled across the scales from the greater spaces—
In Dragoncraft came they,
Came they with emblematic Dragonaxes!—
To found here an isolated colony
Where the long roots end and the earthly waters start.

Now the hammers (dear mother) have danced on their anvils,
There is nothing between our people and the stars.

The bonedance necklaces are flung into the fire
(There is nothing between our people and the stars),
The belles dance naked now
That Dragonshadows fall from the midnight moon.

Today I held your Dragongrandson on my lap.
Touching his leg, I said the immemorial word *shin*.
The model of the bone is millions of years old;
The mother of the word is millions of years old: *shin*.

Our Dragondaughter writes on the altar too:
A poem begins the world and a poem will end it.

Opposable Tongue

Today my tongue could run, though all thumbs, out
Doors of its own making
And talk to plants in their tongue, which can lift weights.

*

The thumb
Locates a path.

In love with the way the world is turning now,
I go out to catch the changes as they come
My way: Big families of diamonds and spades.

*

Shifting hinges sing dry numbers
Until the winds die down and sleep awhile
Without gnashing or rapid eye movement.

*

I don't know how, but the bootless tongue
Goes on anyhow—it may be bad manners—
Opposing the unhappiness it must tell.

I do know this much: sacrifices line the corridor
Reproachfully dictating letters of indebtedness
To civil-service secretaries.

Will I give them my undivided attention?
Not as long as my tongue—

*

Today the envelopes arrive,

Conveniently equipped with windows
That disclose my name and numbered house and town
But keep them safe from
The hundred-year-old mailman's thumb.

He cuts and shuffles, cuts again and deals.
I take a look piecemeal at my new hand.
                                    Sixes! Sevens!

The House

Now the only thing the house has ever really wanted to do is fly, but it is
unable to.
It has wings, east and west, but they are wings of occidental hardwood fastened
to lead beams by means of mortal nails.

The fists of Epictetus come punching through the weak ceiling.
Avuncular knees (they look sneaky, like Calvin's in Geneva) insinuate
themselves through the cracks of vacuum dust.

Spangled shingles shine under the double eagle sun and moon.

Santas violate the flue, detonating the glassware that used to come with the
purchase of eight or more gallons of regular gasoline.
Superposed on Luther's smooth face's five-o'clock shadow, Philipp
Melanchthon's blackened eyes and nose come abruptly up out of the
bathtub, mouthing "ONO."

Again the house tries to lift itself,
But its bones, once light and hollow, have been pumped full of sheetrock and
steel wool.

Even so, the house tries to lift, as in a dream you try to move out of the way of
an oncoming bus but cannot.

That is how the earthbound house will wake up suddenly some nights as
though a storm of leaves and feathers were to stir the waves of the world
with long spoons.

The Window

for Kathleen Norris

Drab a drab morning, and mute, a mockingbird out to know well enough
what's what,

But now, November's end, hunched, shrunk and hungry-looking, in a perfectly
plucked young sycamore

(A bleached tree that seems out of place here among high mighty pines)

At least one looks for all the world as though he were lost.

Our shadows, if we should take that particular path, would become the same as
the sycamore's and his.

Mothsong

Some dust,

such as it is,
is transferred from a mother's album
to a son's turning finger,

then from the finger
to the front of a dark coat,
once a father's,

and then, some months later, from there
to the substance found
on a newborn moth's wing,

witnessed intermittently from below
colliding fitfully with the frosted globe
of a simple fixture
in the middle of a kitchen ceiling,

an irregular but redundant disturbance,
turning, stubborn, a tolling
of sorts, or
a knocking,

like something asymmetrical happening,

the song of an old fork
going, going, gone downstairs.

And so from that moth now
back to this paper—not
so far after all
from the heavy black pages
of a mother's mandatory album under a table lamp,

bland perfunctory public paper
here in the hand,
to be balled up,

a fist, a mind,
a clenched white apple
hanging in a darkening orchard.

By Myself in a Public Park in the Early Morning

I came across a horseshoe among weeds at a big field's edge,
a real one, with holes for nails and slots for countersinking the nails' heads.
I heaved it underhand a hundred feet
to where there was a wooden croquet stake.

With wet rust red on my humming fingers, I was alone;
there was nobody to witness my magnificent ringer,
snugly at rest against the stake's foot, iron to wood,
just as the sun's lower limb lifted from the horizon
as though seized, gripped, filled, taken, inspired mouth-to-mouth.

Noble Achilles of the world-historical shield:
royal Arjuna, peerless archer of the Eighteen Days:
greatest *kshatriya* princes of antiquity: be with me.
Nothing like that will ever happen to me again
at daybreak or any other hour of the day or night.

A Helmet Made of Boar's Teeth

In a particular hatbox—who knows
What has become of the original contents?—
In a hatbox kept in the dark on a high shelf
The helmet smells less year by year
But becomes yellower. It will, by and by,
Be brown, outright, as well as odorless.

An heirloom, it cannot be worn to wars or parties any more
Or taken places as a talisman or mascot.
Each tooth (not counting the four
That are gone absolutely) is loose.

I ought to tell this story to my son:

One night, when I was as happy
As somebody alone and naked is likely to get,
I set it on my head
And walked with dignity down the dim hall
From the closet to the half-bathroom.
There I looked long into the sober mirror.
How the godly split tusks curved every which way!
I bared my own teeth, such as they were then,
And whispered me a pendragon whisper: *Oink*.

If in the beginning they name you William
You have a helmet with you all the time.

Although you can pull snakes' fangs and hypnotize tigers,
Your body will outlast your soul
In more or less the same way that
A hatbox can outlast a hat.

Therefore, I leave—I mean: I hereby will
My temporary teeth to the Masons
(One for each of their ancient thirty-two degrees).

Redounding

Responsively
Our whole house shakes to the thunder's psalm,

Windows react
To the wind's offices, and I am turned all the way around

By the bold sound
That represents, in one sense, almost nothing at all

But, in another sense,
The presence of an old God—popular,

Avuncular,
Gullible, petty, sports-minded, omnipotent, girl-crazy,

But nothing now
But noise, with some nominal vestiges of awe. One

Could tell it to
Roar on. Byron told (James said "besought") the deep blue sea

To roll,
Longfellow told the flower of the lily to bloom on. Romanticism

Did things
Like that. Redundant. So what the hell: throw

Your hammer, Thor!
Thunder, thunder. Be yourself. Provoke apostrophes. That's it.

Thunder Stuns Stutterers Mum
Among Jumbo Doombooms

Dog of the sky barks
Tons of thunder.

Dog of the earth barks back
Tons of nothing-thunder, echoes ago.

All the telephones in the world crow
Like the weak sun above an ice age.

All the starcocks in the equinox sky
Shake angrily their many-colored combs.

Zubby Sutra

(Introduction to a Farewell to Religionswissenschaft)

You know, reading the Bhagavadgita at bedtime can have its drawbacks;
last night, for instance, falling asleep in that ebbing free fall in
wandering mazes of direct or indirect objects lost, I floated undulant
in a kind of zero gravity free-wheeling, wondering why I should wonder
about Gods so much, inasmuch as I seem such a radically secular, casual
character, ascetic of the concrete, kickrock, cardinal in the college of
middleclass suburban bureaucratic skepticism, monk among two-headed
ice-cream cones, partiflavored, anchorless anchorite whose one deep
eventful cave of commitment remains in libidinous perpetuity the
luminous numinous phenomenon of the human female bombshell bosom
(cartoon barbell boobs with pointblank pingpong nipples
a pink that peaks up pink by pink to dots of virgin burgundy);

it occurred, it occurred to such dimmish me that I had been becoming then
that Gods are on this mind of mine
because: *they really exist*; and at just that second something bit me
on the back of the neck: spider, fly, flea, I'll never know
what (Beelzebub?), but that bugbite in the neck of the night woke up a me
trailing clouds of (italicized) a nebulonimbus theology; so

up; down the dark hall into a quick dilation of enamel-linoleum light
in the kitchen I flipflopped to, ate some cheese etc., had me swallows
of some homemade lemonade out of a refrigerated jar, and in the adjacent
dining room looked awhile, minus focus, at the lemuresque me
mothered by the off television screen, our larval lar,
her placid ecru surface bending and returning (cathode, anode,
one: same) my glasses treading their water of air (though
"water" seems too dark a word: say "sea") above my maroon and white
polkadot
summer pajamas awash in a cameo shrapnel of cracker crumbs; quiet

time, me wondering whether to wonder whether some fork-lifting
devil out of one of those endless hells of virtue degree
zero might not have been dispatched as the executing creature that
put the bite on me right on the very verge and brim

of epiphany;
quiet time, our two old cats asleep in the carport, one, the elder,
Pat, a savvy mama cat, the other, her daughter our daughter named Zubby,
much less smart, warped, retarded, or crazed maybe, we speculate, by
having birthed a litter of kittens while still herself hardly more than
a kitten—even so, a nice cat, she (neuter now), sweet-tempered through a
thousand blinking cat-hours of crosseyed bewilderment, fear, nonstop
terror of the bad neighborhood dogs and four-year-old boys
that pull your tail; one day last year I angrily clapped hands, whereupon
a redbird she had captured flew intact out of her mouth; and now, from
the vicinity of the twi-paned storm-door between the dining room
and carport, out of—where? some endopsychic echo-chamber of prehistory?—
    there
spoke a friendly but firm voice: "List here: dumb as she may be,
and there is no doubt in the world that she is just as dumb as they come,
that modest cat a dozen times a day every day blinks blinks
that mean infinitely more to each of the Gods
than all your midnight visions of divinity, all of your horse sacrifices,
basilicas, upanishads, psalms, masses, homiletic ditties, take your pick";

you know, that's some word, that word "polkadot."

Ode

Dawn

yawn. Early birds there where
the lawn got late yestreen mown,
sufficiently scalped for early worms to surface, more hurly
than burly, extra-early, just in time for the Checkerboard farm news
and some enterprising darkling cardinals' prayer breakfast
among dew-dandelions and honeysucklings.

What a lot of bah humbug there is out there in the world today.
Breathing I look uncaring (much) out the window of my room here
giving the old east a look-see:
vagaries, crates, vicissitudes, and crates
red-lettered INDEPENDENT APPLES.
Much geography, little history, some math, zero civics.

A good deal of bah humbug is botany and meteorology
so that about all that I have to want to say here now
is what a fine dandy thing it is that I remain patient
with bah humbug

and as a matter of fact even fond thereof
because if
I should become impatient-with
or contemptuous-of
bah humbug
then (look out), believe you me, the world would be
in big
trouble,
and so would I (in this so lyric fishbowl) be, too.

Accordingly, somewhat in the admirable if naïve manner of Margaret Fuller, I
am in a position to announce—while, figuratively speaking,
flinging wide my hyperkinetic arms—I accept the bah humbug,

because in the absence of it
just what do you reckon there would be?

Let's see:
a cyclone fence and a hurricane lamp, I imagine,
a snow plow and a (metaphoric) storm door, and
a mob of determined morons
bent on retailing me a new mower for my lawn
and a Virgin Mary tumbler for my gone-to-seed toothbrush
to besweeten my fated breath on the way out, its exit stroke,
and O
snapshots by someone—Curt Bruce, that's it—to go with the Gita,
and an eon's supply of a new sleep pill they call Sinequan.
Those guys are going to find full-time work waiting for them in hell,
in the marketing section, thinking up names for newborn demons: Infido,
Yoganil, Placidel, Zeroidin, Quaalude, Seamstench, Carbondale, Nadael. . . .

Without perfunctory universes, furthermore, without the classic kosmoi
of that good old bah humbug, there would be
Scrooge waxing in his old age madly good
and Tiny Tim jammed ex machina athwart his own
lucidly ordained destiny of permanent impotence
and, living unlimping forever, to compete
for all I know
in all the Olympics until
Apocalypse's summa karma kingdom comes,
Indian summer to end all Indian summers.

To all those broadcast-frequency upanishads of bah humbug out the rhyme-
        scheme window, then,
I think I prefer
(for today) the smaller installments of bah humbug
inside,
modest shipments of music via radio, a cake to bake,
furnage to be figured, Saturday cartoons
permitting television to express its essential self
(i.e., cathode, anode, ditto—preSocratic), this wee
ode to breathe out extemporaneous and (a dog watch) type

on what is after all the only really Royal thing in this house,
antique machine in perfect
working
order
though over thirty years old, the dear enigmatic bah humbug
of Q W E R T Y which
is where I conclude
both integumentally and conceptually,

as

a revival preacher, heaven-for-leather
and leather-for-lung,
ought to stop
in his evangelical tracks
when he looks pentecostally down and,
instead of calling for the
sick lame halt deaf dumb and bald of mind
to be healed through grace by faith and all that,

recognizes in a flash (drummerblam) that Paul
was nothing more than a master of business administration
with minors in Greek and retail merchandising, all to all,
crook to the crook, Jew Jew, whereupon scales
of pastoral care drop clamorous
from his missionary eyes
and he says,

"Choir, you hush. Ushers,
stop right now
on that apostolic dime, you there
with those long-handled collection plates
like long spoons for devil dinners.
You saviors and ye saviees, call a halt
to all this
soling of sawdust up and down the carpet
and
with me
see
O
how unutterably jejune and otiose
be all the uses of this bah and humbug world;

and just
cease."

Breathe, brethren,
the fact that a scant handful
of added flats will effect
the modulation from bah humbug
to blah ho hum, as

of
an
August Saturday sort of under-overcast
so that the sun (absconditus)
exhibits roughly as much character
as a vacant-lot second base
in the late innings
of a game transacted, trafficked among American boys
obstreperous as the Epworth Poltergeist—

the present is a present (present);

breathe, brethren, where, among
honeysuck, a jalopy
accomplishes the distinguishing dignity
of both botany and machinery,
by and
by subsiding
into some no-thing's-land of
rust (metal) and
rust (blossom-blight),

a unicorn's skeleton prodigious
among the compounded shadows of an apple-colored rose,

all in the changing shade
of a telepathic oak
telling generations of shadow-tailed squirrels
to bury them acorns deep, boys.

Encomiastic Ode to My Personal Destiny

That chipper
   squirrel jumping faultlessly
from one pine to the next
   holds hands with ghosts
and with the thirty-odd-thousand Gods forcibly
   present in each millimeter of
so urgent a journey
   just as willed and as great on one scale as any

undertaken by Mao or Moses
   or me, standing here on the sloping driveway
looking obliquely up for no reason whatever
   unless it be that this twelve-noon spell
is as it was laid down away back in the beginning of all things
   when it was clearly recognized that
animals stand for immortal souls
   one and all;

I go down the slope to the
   mailbox, and if I
should fail to believe with all my heart that my life
   absolutely requires me to do so then
my foot would never reach the concrete.
   And so what if it doesn't? One of these days
I'm going to drop dead
   on a sidewalk somewhere

and I cannot honestly say I care
   much where or when it happens or
who, if anybody, is there to ask, "Is that
   his hat?"
Well, let the bodily sweatband dam the gutter's
   flux for all it will mean to me,
jumping, as I shall be, more or less faultlessly
   to the neighbor, the next tree.

Totem-Motet

A really large wristwatch
With its crystal shattered
Complicatedly
In many places,
The Atlantic Ocean
Clicks in its compound cell,
Complaining about feeling
Too cooped up, suffering
Fearsome cramps in the main-
Spring, fragile balance
Wheel, and the detaining catch
Of the delicate escapement.
Cracks in the curved crystal
Crack among themselves, not like pistol
Cracks but like religions
Progressively subdividing
Until each child
Is a church unto herself,
Complaining bitterly
About her lot, her allotted slot,
The spot no household compound
Can lift, unless it be
Plain salt water in a beaker
At sea, tipping impromptu
First one way, then another,
Between peril and peril:
The timing mechanism
Of a complicated schism.

Literacy

An Abandoned Ode
        for Max Steele

Poems bore me so much
I have quit worrying about them.
I read, needless to say, a great deal,
But few poems.
                I shall talk to them, for a change,
And tell them that I can see quite through them:
Sleeves cobbled up out of amplified trampolines
Like glass showcases full of glass geese,
Metaphors like successful anacondas
Processing some more or less innocent
Examples of local fauna—enough!

A hundred broken arrowheads
Exhibited in a common cotton coffin:
Who's the muse of museums? Mortalita.

The universe is one long *National Geographic*.
Or else, the universe is one long clothesline
Strung from the front porch of a grocery store
To a coil of *Reader's Digests* ready at the left hand
Of God the Dada Almighty.

The many-colored clothes hang in no wind. Enough.

Prose? Prose, especially Herodotus, I still can
Manage to handle well enough—until, that is,
The proper names start surfacing.
When *Wilbur Bigelow opens the Dutch door* though
I shut the book.

The natural state of books
Is shut, after all,
As of people, asleep. . . .

Let Us Love Prose Awhile

Over flat familiar water, a worn course.

Long sentences put the helmsman to sleep.

He steers perfectly and dreams that he is steering
    perfectly and never talks.

Let us rest in the recognition of having seen every
    single drop of that water already.

Danang—Spring MCMLXXV

Our archers are combing out their beautiful shoulder-length white hair.
No.
Our fusiliers are combing out their long hair in the moon's light.
No.
Midnight approaches, moonlight spreads over the camp, our halberdiers comb
    out their beautiful white hair.
No.
The fires die, shadows shorten, our grenadiers comb out their long white hair.
No.
Lancers laugh, the last fire reflected from the silver fillings in their long white
    teeth as they comb out their beautiful hair.
No.
Our bombardiers move in the dark and in the moon's secondhand light,
    combing their white hair.

No.
The personnel of our army are not old enough to have to comb long white
    hair.
Their hair is neither long nor white.
It is something I have seen in dreams only,
A vision of Mediterranean harquebusiers combing out long beautiful white hair
    by the light of a full moon
On the eve of a great historic battle.

No.
Not in dreams but only in museums have I seen the archaic weaponry.
Moonlight in a museum will slide pieces of whiteness along the edges of
    halberds and arrowheads,
Each old edge like a long old white hair, shining.

No, that too is wrong.
What I see is what I see in books,
Their rows of black words nothing like white hair,

The record of the war I was in
Nothing like the archival history of dragoons.

I battled bedbugs in a twice-named city, which now they say has fallen to the
     enemy on the news,
The rows of black words nothing like white hair
Looking more or less unreal under moonlight in the dead center of the
     dreamed night.

The Wings of the Dove

Such suspense seems so peaceful
we fall asleep

and in dreams read the opening passage
over and over: *She waited* . . . .

We wonder who she is
and what she waits for.

To Suffer

The moon reflected in a heifer's eye
    Suffers a change of phase from half to full
      Then back again slowly from full to half,
    While in her womb the image of the bull
      Becomes the image of their coming calf,
A moon repeated in the mother's eye.

Autumnal Colloquy

1.

What makes you think I care
What you did last summer?

2.

What did you do
Last summer? Me too.

Table Manners

Table manners are so emotional!
These knives reflect the teeth they imitate,
Returning us to an uncultured state.

The duke across from me is very tall,
But not so tall as Dottie (my blind date).
    Table manners are so emotional
      These knives reflect the teeth they imitate.

The seamstress next to me is very small
And talks a jargon I could learn to hate
(Sharp scissor images predominate).
    Table manners are so emotional.
      These knives reflect the teeth they imitate,
      Returning us to an uncultured state.

Sentimental Etude on Dogeared Foolscap

Actually Succotash can skate without collapsing
And knows full well what cool to do
In the furnace face of a berserk bull. At home
He has a closet of conventional clothing,
Not those bulb-toed exophthalmic saddle oxfords two feet long
In high-shine purple and yellow
And no helium-ballooning trousers with a hula-hooping
Sixty-inch waistline twice too big.

He has eight real hats
With no floral tributes wandering forlornly from the crown;
His actual hair is nothing remotely like royal blue
In a gas-burner fringe crowned around a steep pate
The actual color of "green" cheese (which is moon-white).

He is said to dive straight as a die from unearthly heights
Like an Olympic medalist, ski like mad or anything, swim
Endlessly, swallow swords, produce presto a full deck
From thin air or your ear, eat fire from a short spoon,
Geronimo nonchalantly out of barrel-rolling Cessnas, and
With a quelling gesture that marries modesty to understanding
Coax inflamed tigers into supine docility.

Even so, the little dotted dog does not really belong to him.
The disorderly sock drawer at home (he owns a mobile home)
Does hold a joke or two of the second or irregular persuasion.
Even in plainclothes, it is true, he may sport
One wide tie across which tricky matrix
Polar dots polka with askew Saturns, snapdragons,
Radioactive macaroni marbled like scar tissue
Along a long tongue issuing Jackobox
Out of the apocalyptic gape
Of a nightmare quagmire gone quite ape.

They say Succotash's wife has a crush on a weightlifter
(THE VERY STRONG MAN KWASIND) whose mere gaze,
Even in repose,
Can drown full-grown bullmoose in lagoons of swamping terror
And frantic panic while simultaneously prompting substantial deputies
To turn their badges back in
Just on the basis of hearing gossip about how he breakfasts.

But actually Succotash can act in the classics handsomely.
He has been Macbeth in Akron and Duluth,
As well as a "highly convincing" Philoctetes in El Paso.
His is a trained tenor voice
Utterly different from the twisted rustic tongue
Falling flat over the threshold of such obstacles as "Schenectady."
He'll sing "Here I Stand with One Foot in the Grave" by Bach.

From her sphere of mantic crystal, yonder Magyar woman knows
That there is a night going to fall
When he will not be able to skate without collapsing
And he will fail to repeat after the patient nurse,
"Sphygmomanometer."
He really will not know whose head is on the Lincoln penny
Or who is buried in Grant's Tomb.

But that's to come. For now, rejoice
That he does hold an Oxford doctorate and can juggle
These dozens of incandescent butcher knives without letting a one
Fall through the huge shoe that is reflecting many colored footlights
In curved figures that may be, after all,
Melodramatic facsimilies of smiles.

The Lilies of the Field Know Which Side
Their Bread Is Buttered On

Clear as a bell, the substantial summer night rings with many hymns.

Mindlessly, a million singing insects obey the dictates of instinct.

Nor cloud nor moon obstructs the space that supervenes between each singing
    thing and each circling star.

Swastika stars, Siberian stars, science-fiction stars. . . . I ought to be in bed
    asleep. I ought to be in bed.

3:30 a.m., 73°. Thanks, clock; thank you, motherly thermometer.

And thank you, insects. You must know a million things, and I may know a
    million million,

But what is that? What difference could that make

Compared to all of the infinitely subdivided infinities

Deep inside each spontaneous antique atom of your song, each significant air
    and articulated rhythm, each phrase, item?

A dog, near by, barks once.

A far dog barks in answer, or as though in answer.

(Geckoes' echoes, letter perfect.)

Now they fall silent. A set of insect strings or membranes assumes a new
    network of music, musics.

Something, truck-like, hums,

Hums lower, then shifts deeper and goes on in a heavy-duty register, far away.

Some mourning dove or owl donates notes to the orchestra's chord. In light
    pajamas, on our front porch, I wonder what in the world is going on

In the world.

Strolling-while-leaning, one of the cats draws by, putting a lot of confident self-
    indulgent pressure on the backs of my naked ankles, idly seeking company
    and pleasure.

Who knows? The sun may not come up at all this morning,

In which case, cat, the lilies of the field will turn out to have been right all
    along.

The truck's pedal point is heard no more. We were a passacaglia, cat. Retail
    merchandising made this country great. Light travels light.

I think I would be better off illiterate again.

Reading Freud for hours on end has reduced my dreams to such ridiculous
    rubble.

Imagine me—also the year 1899 incarnate—at an Austro-Hungarian costume
    ball sporting a bearded mask of pasteboard

With a bakelite caption, "1900." . . . Now that's really dumb.

Well, what an amiable beast of burden I must be, to sit here, an oh-so-sensitive
    being being oh-so-sensitive,

One petty officer in the ancient and more or less honorable company of the
    world's poets, composing,

While out there in the Christlike darkness there throbs a country of mortgages,

A vast magnificent civilization founded on retail merchandising,

Every man a middleman, every beast, even, a middlebeast.

I bark a bit myself, inside. The insects' number is beyond me.

Listen: there used to be a verse in the book of Ezekiel,

One of those wonderfully overstated mosaic rhapsodies of gorgeous mockery
addressed to poor old ruined Tyre:

The suburbs shall shake at the sound of the cry of thy pilots.

Or words to that effect, something like that, prepositional triads wall-to-wall,
hot-and-cold-running alliteration and internal rhymes, Dark Age verb
forms.

The verse may be there yet, for all I know.

Even if I weren't scared to death to open that black Jacobean book, though, it
would still be too dark to read.

Even so, if starlight, doglight, catlight, buglight, nightlight, whatever, were
enough to see by, I would make it out there, in good order,

The twenty-seventh chapter and the twenty-eighth verse: *suburbs, pilots,* just
like now.

And the language so grand that Kipling could speculate that Shakespeare had
had a hand in it.

Pilots, not a mile from here at an airport named for a philosophy professor,

Or over yonder where the modern Lebanese are flattening their Tyre again.

But the wreckage and the prophet's mantic number remain beyond me.

Yawn.

They're burning the thermometer at both ends nowadays, and I certainly ought
to be in bed asleep.

But something from the Golden Age lodges in my wake. Long ago, when I was
a child, able to sleep all night every night,

They used to write scriptures out in sacred radium that glowed in the very dark,

Perfect letters on a lurid blue background with sprinklings of silver.

On an old clock there would glow pea-green hands and numerals, mysterious.

If I should die before I wake / I pray the Lord my soul to take. . . .

They've cut that out now, they've quit all that, for safety's sake, the letters and
numerals of faint fire.

Where Scars Come From

To lie down and sleep with the dead for good:
That is what sleeping simply
Comes down to. To sleep with the dead
Is what doing anything is,
And coercively so: necromancy, necking,
Painting an old wooden door red, washing your bare hands,
Inhaling to erase your utterly perishable voice,
Stones tossed, thrown across a pond
Into the shadowed wood beyond.

I got these scars from a dog.
I got this scar in a dream.
I got this scar from a cigar.
This scar I was born with.
I got this scar preparing for a track meet.
I got this scar from a childhood disease.
I have forgotten how I got this one.
I got this scar from a can-opener
And this one next to it from a grenade-launcher.

Naked, I am Everyman: bilateral, diurnal,
Pedestrian, rhythmic, superstitious, and—like the occluded God
Of the witch-doctor or modern theologian—awful.

I got these parallel scars from one oven.
I got this series of scars from a steam-line on a destroyer.
I got this scar from a hawk-bill knife.
I got this scar from a kitchen knife.
I got this scar from sodium trichloro-acetate.
I got this scar from a fire
And this scar from a fish.

I know when I sleep that I lie down with the dead
And I know what it is to sleep with them,
With my father and his father and his father

And the solid succession of mortal fathers
Link by link back through thousands and thousands of seasons.
I fear them as tearfully
As I would have feared them before death;
Even so, how can I keep from sleeping?
To sleep at all is to sleep with all of them
Down in the dormitory of the dead, one long poem: the fathers,
Mothers, sisters, brothers, friends,
All people
And all flamboyant animals and hapless plants.

This scar I got from the innocent-looking edge of a piece of paper.
I got these scars from myself (a mistake).
I got this scar chopping wood with the *Iliad* in my blood.
I got this particular scar, and this, and this,
And this circle of satellite scars, from a team of surgeons.
Don't touch.
This looks like a scar but isn't.
I remain (my darlings, my dying darlings) at a loss to account for it.

The Elementary Inventions of the Species

Rote: a raw sad noise not your own voice, racket
Of a peculiarly articulated grief
On account of the woeful slaughter of some unimportant stranger
At a barbaric place where three low roads meet;

Obscene giggle, chatter
From the notorious dormitory of hierodules and screwballs
Loose, careening bestially through an unmonitored night
Brandishing outlandish wine-dark artificial genitalia;

An unprompted something from the old throat of a mother
All in mourning black among nomad orphans
Packing up to move to winter pasture
At the far edge of a province indifferently governed by a pickpocket;

Or: nothing if not the cry of an infant outraged,
Naked at noon among aloof infidels
Who lack any notion of magic or religion
And have never yet mastered the use of salt or metal,

No anthem but these words sung over and over on two notes:
Growing old, going home, the same, the same.

Low Comic Requiem Mass for Loners and Exiles

What if one take the lightning by the horns,
Or govern like a godly governor?

Scorched, smothered,
Song (under megatonnage of bass brasses brazenly
Out-uttering one another bell by bell) tolls
Goodly-good good-bye, so, so, so long

With every bit of metered dignity
Permitted by celestial abruptness
As it subtends our arc.

Our Lady of the Succotash:

The brownly bearish church will have shrunk a mote,
The dogwood may not bark through the same throat.
Thus drags the ho-hum drama down to drumroll.

Circumferences of canonical cathedrals crown
The plumb evacuated skull of Edgar Poe with asymmetric lights
Collected from all mornings, noons, and nights
And recollected in a pickpocket's pocket.

A Dog Named for My First Blind Date

1

Dispossessed, arrows of longing, we tender our hands
For love of the other shore.

Templum temporis, pure amplitude
Only minutely diminished by being temporary:

One sunset as sentimental as a Balkan banknote,
Another resembling a really busy beach,

Horizontal echelons, robust with blue plus red
There, there, and there gold-machicolated,

Coronets of sunlight in nets,
A cornet's dwell-time on one note of honey or money.

2

No sun now, and Barbara Marshall
Is barking the backyard to bits
All through her oracular night
Until the guest stars, in no wise standing upon the order
Of their galactic going, take their unreluctant leave;

And she will burn her morning off
With many barkings, preSocratic aloha shirts of basic racket
Cauterizing every silent entity in sight.

3

Dear Barbara: sweetheart: bark my aching mortal back
From Aeneas to Zarathustra and back again:
Aren't you in on every mystery and instinct,
The secrets of animal character, the barbaric past,

The fundamentals of the female temperament,
One's vacant alien bestial taboo piety after death?

Three months ago
You were a foetus, one of fourteen
Lodged inside a single heroine.

4

O my sibylline retriever, golden, cordial—actually
The pup's name is just Sadie.
I imagined all that poluphloiosboiotatotic *dadadás*
Of the world's one ocean concentered in each paradigmatic decal,

And didn't I just make up all that logico-philosophicus stuff
About Barbara Marshall,
The living girl who swapped throats with a dog?

And "Le Tombeau" Glows in Another Dark

The field of vision yields a figure of pure fire
Edged with nocturnes and penumbrae, blue and black:

Poe,
Demon to the demon of himself, self-forking
Into a tolling groan and telling diabetic brief
As though from the underworld to America.

Retail merchandising made this country what it is.

Ours is a magnificent civilization and this our Golden Age,
Thanks in part
To Poe's having worked himself to death by forty.
After his miserable Baltimore October death,
It was twenty-six years before the filled hole
Bore any proper stone,

Whitman the diplomat with nothing to say,
And from polar Mallarmé
A religious figure of speech

As though to accompany one on a short barge-ride to hell,
Perfunctory enigma.

Go, Bid the Soldiers Shoot

While in a spell of sane commemoration
Let them commemorate the mad Franz Lipp,
People's Commissar for Foreign Affairs
In Communist Munich in 1919.

Lipp quoted Kant in a telegram to Lenin
And reported: "Liberal bourgeoisie completely
Disarmed as Prussian agents. The cowardly Hoffmann
In his flight took away the key to my W.C."

What world is what it was and as we are?
As it is what we were and as we see
And, insofar as we can see, as far?
Lipp filled the secretaries' room with red carnations.

Stevens

Memorial umbrellas congregate
Among the ordnance and brides of edgy banjos
Whose randy badinage lifts saffron mangoes

Through reefs of leaves dressing a green nadir.
Theatric thunders in their ithyphallic laundry-theater
Thumb through rolls in the blue world's doomsday books

Looking for names to name and number and numb.
They named his name once on a tomb who now
Would number us in the barrel of lumber-blossoms

Not yet bitch-bitten. Lullabies abound,
However; lullabies proliferate;
And memoranda, blissful memoranda,

Enough to stuff a grandiose caboose.

Auden

Already the routine ritual paragraphs appear,
    Prefabricated obituaries that distort
Important names and transpose dates and continents
    Until the modest busy life is modified
Into a civic fiction, as false as the photograph
    Becomes to the face, as the poet's body, untended
For a day or two, will become to the unkept spirit.

    Sit still: we are ready because he readied us,
Delivering for forty years the old homily,
    That the human business of poetry is human business—
Not ego-flattering or self-pity or any other squalid
    Cheap operation of Personality, but rather
The sort of act most prosaic and most difficult:
    To take note, pay attention, and remember.

Grammar (the science of fun and the moon) regards
    In gross accustomed springs and autumns
The didactic cadences, fresh and radiant, of
    Antic-antique syntax radically irregular but right
For charismatic archaisms, musical tools, articles
    Of machinery and faith, imaginary
Universes organized as madly formal gardens

        Whose harvest feeds
        Our extravagantly
        Unkempt hungers.

Berryman

Well. I guess the elegy is dead. If so, then
let's let it roll to rest-o. Exeunt omnes. Ergo,
timor mortis conturbat
mé tóo, I reckon. Oh I get such green-edged vertigo
as the sick poet must have on the quickly lifting
bridge's shift of footing, or leaning peaked up above the grave
of his felo de se of a father down
in unlikely Oklahoma

(or wherever) toward the lower end of the fatherly
river, the bottom of the one old brown bottle
too. Christ. There is just not enough skin to go around,
not enough foolscap for the roll
of poets and fathers down the hatch of an
overdose of one thing or another,
not enough words. They fall behind and fall,
and love and fame to nothingness do sink. Kéats.

We owe, I said, some words to our dear brothers dead
under the waters of our brother sea
or brotherly river, involuntarily long with elegies
turning the swollen helmet-hubs of hearses into mud.
The vehicles get no rest and never will, I
guess, until there's nobody left to steer
the lást óne, the day—part of this single ugly winter night
we constitute the punctuation of, the temporary commas—the day

when the one surviving bridge-enduring poet
must tie with cold fingers his even colder tie
and roll then himself unaided and alone
down the dim hill to the darkling hole,
releasing
the emergency brake
and letting the neutral gears
go wheeling free.

The Twentieth Century

These things are real, children:
Who needs to make things up?

Houston Stewart Chamberlain,
Wagner's son-in-law, hailed
Hitler as the new Savior.

Baron Roman von Ungen-Sternberg,
Wedded to a Mongolian princess,
Rode a horse dragging
Human torches through darkness.

Interoffice Memorandum to James Seay

(In memory of Lee Anderson Pickerel, 1881–1976)

Great age came down on Lee
Like a gradual fall of small flakes, cancellations
That chipped his speech, depressed
His head, erased much of his memory.

I happened to be setting out, when he reached eighty,
For a three-year tour of Navy duty
In the Pacific. Although a native Virginian,
He was never to set eyes on even the Atlantic.
He held his deciduous hand up and out to me
And said I probably wouldn't be seeing him again.

Three years later I passed through Virginia
En route from one snakeless island to another,
Pearl Harbor to Londonderry,
And held the same changing hand. Two years after that,
Passing from Europe through America to Asia, to Vietnam,
I stopped by his house again. Having seen
Two sons off to war a generation earlier,
He now held out his hand to a grandson bound somehow
For the same mysterious oriental distances, dim.
A westward journey takes us to "the East,"
Where English breaks into flakes and burlesques.

Back home again after a solid year of not getting killed,
I called on him. Hands . . . you know the rest.

One time I asked him if tobacco farming paid well.
"Hush," he said; "one year I made *seven hundred dollars.*"

The family gathered for his ninetieth.
He held up his hand—nails clipped, a dignified irregular range
Of large rough knuckles—but I kissed the cheek instead
And told him he would bury me. His wife had died

The year before, and he would say,
"I never did treat Sal right."
I said that he had been married to her for sixty-eight years
And if that wasn't enough chance to treat her right
There sure wasn't much damned use worrying about it now.
I changed the subject to our shared "male pattern baldness,"
Which, sex-linked, was coming to me through my mother's family
And had come to him through his mother's family. Pretty soon
We would be able to comb our heavy eyebrows up and back
And cover up our matrilinear pates. I was getting earbrows, too,
Like his. "You've got more hair in your right ear," I told him,
"Than I've got on my whole head, you rascal."

I was there (Motley community, near Hurt,
Pittsylvania County) for his ninety-fifth.
He exhaled eleven or twelve treasured breaths
Through his trembling harmonica, surprisingly *presto*.
One of my aunts said, "Dad, play 'Home Sweet Home.'"
He said, "I just did."

To buy useful presents for him had become impossible.
And he loved presents, even the odd dollar
Folded inside a meretricious greeting card—
One of those lurid paradigms of retail insincerity
With the cretinous versicles *so* profoundly offensive
To genuinely authentic poets, like you and me.
He needed nothing any of us could come up with.
Then, for some reason, by a tacit or explicit conspiracy
That embraced even the great-*great*-grandchildren,
We settled on two recurrent sorts of gift:
Cardigan sweaters of every style and color
To keep the cold away (and he always felt cold)
And the gaudiest toiletries: pre-shave,
After-shave, cologne, some
With sadistically distinguished names
Like *English Leather*, some others
Fantastically exotic for Motley, near Hurt, Virginia:
Jade East, Hai Karate. . . .
I don't suppose he had the dimmest idea
What karate means. (I don't suppose I do, either.)
My mother and I were of the cardigan party.

Well, Jim—to make a long story short—he died,
And in the hundred dosidos and shuffles over "property"
(Nothing more than a four-room frame house
And a rock-laced acre of land) I wound up
With eight or ten cardigans
And about a dozen bottles of masculine cosmetics—
Decanters speaking of nautical smartness, brisk and bracing,
Bottles shaped like antique cars or light bulbs,
God knows what all, mad capricious surreal things, outlandish.
Luckily, when I got home I accidently dropped one whole paper sack
And got rid of half of the tacky things in one stroke
Right in my own concrete driveway, which smelled of Midnight in Manila
For a whole week. The very air—a *tour de Brut force*—shimmied.
I don't use such stuff, myself,
Except to sniff at now and then
When reorganizing the contents of the medicine cabinet.

But all of this does do one thing, my friend. It makes me think
That you and I had better think twice
Before we get too glib in telling those dreadful desperate students
Of ours in Creative Writing (P) (for Poetry)
How high and mighty sick and tired We are of falling leaves
And fractured hearts and how We—such big Wesleyan et cetera deals—
Do not want to see
Any more corny free-verse meditations on somebody's
Rustic grandfather's hands.

Yours in Mississippi gave you a pocket knife
And then became forgetful and pestered you about it.
Mine left me a drawer full of sweaters with pockets
And a shelf of fluid rubbish, largely green.
I wear the sweaters now and then
Even though they scarcely fit my figure or the fashion.
At present I have no plans to use the scents,
But I am going to hang on to them anyway,
At least for a while.

I suppose my maternal grandfather—Mr. Lee Anderson Pickerel—
Until the day he died
Regarded the wristwatch, the belt, the cigarette,
And the low-cut shoe (or "slipper")
As sure signs of fecklessness and city ways.

He might have thrown away the toiletries, too—
They say he had no use for flowers in any form—
If he could have found a courteous way to do so.

Still, Jim, for the sake of our self-respect
And the sacred honor of our atavistic art, let's continue
To act as vigilant watchdogs flanking the doors
Of the temple of poetry
Lest some profanely sentimental immature undergraduate
Tries to slip by our fangs and F's
And sneak in with some cheap shot
(All lower-case egomania and misspelled platitudes)
About the spots and palsies afflicting the poor old hands
Of his or her God-damned grand-dad
Growing old and dying in the God-damned sticks
Some forsaken place in our South—one of those shrimp villages
Ulcering up the coast or picturesque settings
In the hills or mountains
Among the innumerable God-damned falling leaves
                                                        of
                                            autumn,

Autumn.

The Chariot

Memento mori? Good God: as though he could forget—
His father has been dead for thirty years,
For thirty-five his younger brother dead,
His best man wasted eleven years ago
In a war (one random mortar round
Chucked into downtown Saigon on some holiday
Exploded next to him, decked out in dress whites—
A blaze of complete whiteness broken only
By the brass buckle on his starched-stiff web belt,
The black-and-gold commander's shoulder boards,
And the brass-and-silver eagle-anchors-shield
Device on the cap above the gold chin-strap),
A couple of infarcted uncles, one poor aunt
Blitzed bald by cancer treatments, one leg left. . . .

It makes him quit imagining, makes him admit
That he is I.
          My son's name is my father's,
Word for word, and that formal Roman "II"
Collects me into recollection.
                    That, and this:
Although at times whole days or even weeks go by
With no hint of the dead, there come some nights
With storms of dreams like showers of shooting stars,
They are alive, they never have been dead
And cannot understand why I should be so happy—
My father at his best, a striking man
Affectionate and generous as music
(Back in the Twenties he had led a dance band),
My brother, whom I've never seen at all,
Is here, is whole, sharing jokes and secrets,
Commander Richard Edris in those damned dress whites,
A silver holder for his cigarette
(For he was genuinely elegant,
Even in the jungle in a combat zone),

Appraising C-rations like some *haute cuisine*,
The beans and franks *splendide,* the turkey loaf less so,
The toilet paper worth at least four stars
Itself to round a meal off with that cultured
Touch, all of us in stitches. . . .

He wakes from such spells feeling strange all over
It's no use trying to get back to sleep.
The clock's fuse fusses near its charge. Sun rise
With worlds of nonchalant magnificence
And infinite originality;
The wife and children stir, the percolator sighs, exhales
(A noise his father always loved to listen to),
The chariot with wings retreats
And rises out of sight
If never out of mind, at least not quite.

There

for my daughter and son

Somewhere, then—the bottom
Of the ocean, the middle
Of the air, the end of the earth,
Tundra, steppe, oasis—
Maybe very far away
But probably close to home here,
There waits a special place mentioning my name,

Not what you call me
When we eat a meal or trim a tree
But that which one is called
By the unending law, one's full name,

Its formal arrangement of ancestral phonemes designed after all
Finally to be dismantled by whatever
Whim motivates whatever veering or backing wind—

Typhoon, simoon—

And maybe some day to be reassembled
Altogether by accident, for twenty seconds
Or so,
Every totemic syllable miraculously intact

And registered prismatically in the precinct
Of a writing spider or hermit crab
Making its mortal way from one meal to the next,

Until a shift of wind will lift
It and create something else
Out of it, scruple by scruple, somebody else's name
Or number: that, say,
Of a dumb animal
Seated at a hypothetical keyboard
In a proverbial laboratory
Depressing one character after another

Until by the law of averages the imperial tissues of Lear
Are stretched out yet one more time
Upon the radioactive rack of this tough world,
A house like ours goes spinning around
Among the particolored science-fiction stars—
Tundra, steppe, oasis, simoon, typhoon—and
Tick, tick, tick, your names are typewritten too;

Then the voices of two special spaces
Hollowed out by the unending law
To take your neat names in a perfect fit
Will whisper, "That's it," and "That's it."

When It Comes

for Norman Maclean

What does it all come down to when it comes?
How do things end that have the grace to end?
The *Iliad* stops with "Hector the breaker of horses";
The last word of *Lord Jim* is "butterflies."